Healing Emotional Wounds

Ruth Hawkey

New Wine Press

New Wine Press
PO Box 17
Chichester
England PO19 2AW

Unless otherwise stated, all Scripture quotations are taken from the New
King James Version, copyright © 1983 by Thomas Nelson, Inc.

Amplified Bible Old Testament, copyright © 1965, 1987 by the
Zondervan Corporation. The Amplified New Testament, copyright ©
1957, 1987 by the Lockman Foundation. Used by permission.

ISBN: 1 874367 87 6

Typeset by CRB Associates, Reepham, Norfolk.
Printed in Malta

Contents

Preface

Emotional wounds go very deep and can cause serious heart-ache within a person, which can last for years. Whilst such wounds may not be able to be seen, nevertheless it is true to say that they certainly can be felt. Jan was only twenty-seven years old, recently divorced and heading for a nervous breakdown; her doctor had tried tablets, a psychologist and the local hospital but all to no avail, for there are no tablets that can be prescribed for a broken heart. The reason for her brokenness was not that her husband had divorced her after six years of marriage, but rather that he had deserted her in preference for her best friend. 'It was the betrayal,' she said, 'which caused the deepest cut of all.'

Bob too suffered from painful emotional wounds but for a different reason. He was thirty-two years old and had never had a girl-friend, let alone been married, and that was his problem: his singleness and consequent loneliness. It was the reason why he often lay awake at nights asking himself the same questions over and over again: 'What is wrong with me?' 'Why do women not find me attractive?' 'Why am I still alone and facing forty without hope?' He felt that the years were hastening on and the likelihood of a wife and a family was swiftly passing him by. It wasn't for lack of opportunity but rather the dreadful, controlling, inhibiting, shyness with which he had been cursed since he was a young lad of ten. It was at that age that his mother had totally embarrassed him in front of his new girl-friend at school by insisting that he give her a kiss goodbye, much to the amusement of the other parents standing watching.

Claire also longed to be married, but she had spent much of her life looking after her mother, who was in the early stages of Alzheimer's disease, and now marriage was a very unlikely possibility. The emotional wounding of 'lost hope' cut to the very heart of her, but very few people recognised her deep pain of unfulfilled longings. Space prohibits me from telling the stories of John, Elsie, Frank and hundreds of others who are also suffering from the pain of emotional wounds, but for a number of different reasons, some of which we will consider in the following chapters.

A team of people will spend many hours in an operating theatre putting a broken body back together again. Days of specialised recuperation and months of skilled rehabilitation, even years of repeated operations may follow and are willingly given. But what of a broken heart? People who are emotionally bound, living in a straitjacket of fear and loneliness, crying tears no one else sees, or even cares about. What if such people are in the Church family?

Many people in the Body of Christ are inflicted with what numerous physicians would call an 'untreatable malady', but one which is totally treatable by the Lord; that is, the pain of unresolved emotional wounding or the healing of a broken heart. Part of Jesus' job description is that He came 'to heal the brokenhearted,' and if that is you, then take courage, for He is able to help you, no matter what has brought about your emotional pain or for how many weeks, months, or years you have suffered. One lady said that she had known brokenness for almost eighteen years, before she realised that Jesus could help her.

Jesus clearly saw salvation as a fully rounded thing; to Him it was more than forgiveness, it included freedom, healing, wholeness and maturity. For Jesus, assuming the mantle of Messiah meant taking up the full job description of preaching, healing people and setting them free. He could no more envisage going back to heaven having not healed, than returning to His Father having not preached the Good News, for they were two sides of the same coin to Him.

This book has been written for those who want to under-stand some of the roots of their own brokenness and emotional pain, as well as for those who might be feeling God's call to assist Him in binding up those who are wounded and bleeding on the inside. Father God heard the heartbeat of our pain and came down, in His son Jesus, to deliver us, to heal and to restore us to health and wholeness. Some of us within the Church will have the privilege of being called and equipped to work with Him in that task.

Some people, who have listened to our teaching on 'Healing Emotional Wounds' or 'Healing the Brokenhearted', have requested to have it in written form, for future reading and reference. This booklet is the result of those requests and we trust that it will be a help to the Body of Christ and a means of healing to those whose hearts are sore and wounded.

In the following chapters we will be looking at some of the **roots of brokenness**; the dull ache and pain from loss and separation; the tearing apart of painful relationships; the shame and guilt of abuse, sin and trauma; as well as the agony of being abandoned, rejected and lonely. We will also consider our **reactions to brokenness** (both godly and ungodly) and how Jesus comes **to restore the broken** through His work on the **Cross**. Finally, we will look at some pointers as to how to **minister to the broken and lead them into the place of restoration**.

Chapter 1

Roots of Brokenness – Loss

Loss Situations

There are many situations throughout life, which will have the potential of causing a person to suffer from a broken heart, and because we are all unique, what may break the heart of one person will simply scratch the surface of another. We will consider for a moment the situations in which **loss** may be concerned, for this is one of the key reasons why people will experience the deep emotional pain of guilt, anger or grief, that can result in acute damage on the inside. This loss may be, but doesn't have to be, the death of a loved one. Any kind of situation which involves losing something or someone of importance, has the potential of causing deep grief, wounding and brokenness of heart and this loss can spring from many and varied sources. For example, whilst it may be the result of the death of a person whom one has loved dearly, it may also be because one has been deprived of a career which has given a person status and a meaning to life.

The most common loss, of course, is that which many people are subject to, and to which we have already referred, that of **bereavement** or **separation** from a loved one. Jacob the Patriarch knew something of this when he was told that his son Joseph was dead.

> *'And all his sons and all his daughters arose to comfort him; but he refused to be comforted, and he said, "For I shall go down into the grave to my son in mourning." Thus his father wept for him.'*
> (Genesis 37:35)

It was only when he heard that Joseph was indeed alive that:

> *'The spirit of Jacob their father revived.'* (Genesis 45:27)

I am reminded of the deep sorrow of Bob and Margaret, a lovely Christian couple who were a tremendous blessing within their local church, and the pain and bewilderment which they felt when their sixteen-year-old daughter Frieda died of leukaemia. She was an only child and one can only imagine their pain, their sense of anger and isolation. The death of their child was followed a few months later by the untimely death of Bob himself. Margaret still maintains that he died of a broken heart and that like Jacob, he went down into his grave mourning.

Separations

Separation from a loved one, especially at key times, can almost be as devastating a loss as bereavement. One lady told me of the time she was put on a plane to Canada as a little girl of five or six, during the last war, to stay with her relatives in Ontario. Her parents convinced themselves that they were doing it for the best, in order to save her from the terrible bombing which was taking place at the time in London, but to such a shy and timid child it was like being excommunicated. She told me that she cried for days and days, and every night she would long for her mummy or daddy to turn up and take her home, which they never did, for unfortunately they were both killed in an air raid, shortly after she was flown out to Canada. Her relatives, wisely or unwisely, decided not to tell her of their deaths until she was old enough to understand! Meanwhile the little girl made a decision and a vow that she would never trust or love anyone again.

Unfulfilled Hopes – Childlessness

Any shattering or deferment of hope can also cause emotional wounding. This appears to be especially true concerning the longing for a child, as this can go very deep, both with the husband as well as the wife. Hannah knew something of this deferment of hope as she realised that her longing for a family, a child of her own, was unlikely to be fulfilled.

> *'And she was in bitterness of soul, and prayed to the Lord and wept in anguish.'*   (1 Samuel 1:10)

I have known and ministered to many men and women, in whose grieving hearts lie hidden the deep desire to bring forth a child. For example, I will never forget the look of deep grief on the face of the fifty-year-old lady who fled from the room in which we were taking a seminar on 'Healing the Brokenhearted'. She escaped into the garden in floods of tears, caused by thinking about and facing afresh, the pain of the lost hopes of the years; hopes for a child which would never now be realised. It was just too much to bear. Alongside the hope had grown an accumulation of 'months of maybe'; maybe this time we'll conceive; maybe this time it will work; maybe this time we will be lucky. Many months and years of looking for medical help only compounded this. A hope raised and hopes dashed, month after month and year after year. As I sat and shared with this dear lady in the garden, I realised that she had not been healed from the pain, she had simply dug a grave and buried it. Consequently she had suffered a great deal, both emotionally and physically from the consequences of that 'funeral' of lost hope; sleepless nights, migraines, severe indigestion, as well as irritable bowel syndrome. (This is not to suggest that everyone with the above physical symptoms is nursing a broken heart, but certainly buried emotions can have a physical outworking.)

People who are longing for children and have not conceived, may from time to time also suffer from the insensitivity of some folk who are fortunate enough to have children. This can also hurt and crush the hearts of the childless. For example, an insensitivity in forever talking about the delights of children, around those who haven't any, as well as the assumption that 'Oh well, Mary is a career woman and she doesn't want children.' Or worse still, 'Well they are probably having problems in their marriage and that's why they haven't any kids.' Sometimes it is assumed, within society and the Church, that men are not as affected as women by their lack of having a family. Nothing could be further from the truth, for many a man portrays the 'stiff upper lip' image in order to help and strengthen his wife, while all the time his heart is bleeding also.

Unfulfilled Hopes – Singleness

For some people being single is something to celebrate and rejoice in, for they see it as a great blessing from God – indeed as great a blessing as being married. As single people they are able to grasp the many opportunities which singleness provides. They are free to travel, visit friends, go where the Lord wants them to go, be available and flexible. However for others it is a continuous festering world of pain, which is irritated and opened up whenever the question of singleness arises. This can happen whenever they feel excluded or are faced by the inevitable 'couple' or 'family' situation, which highlights their own pain.

Loss of, or a Failed Ministry

A failed ministry, as was true in the life of Judas, or a **loss** of vision, as happened to Elijah, results in the heartfelt cry, echoed no doubt by many another:

> *'I alone am left; and they seek to take my life.'*
>
> (1 Kings 19:10)

The loss can be just as shattering to their families as it is to the person concerned, as they suffer deeply with them. We have sat with, wept and prayed for, a number of pastors and leaders who have suffered a lot of heartache, because they have destroyed or lost their ministry and thus their future. Sometimes the cause has been due to their own failings and shortcomings, but most often it is due to a number of factors outside of their control. For example, the heartbroken pastor who watched as half of his congregation was taken away from him by an over-enthusiastic youth pastor. The result in this man's life and in the life of his family was devastating.

I well remember the day when a vicar, a lovely Christian man, sat with his head in his hands in our study, weeping uncontrollably, with great heaving of his shoulders, because he had thrown away his ministry for a moment of madness and adultery. How vulnerable are our leaders when they fail and how much greater the judgement against them seems to be, but they are also human and they bleed and hurt as we do; their hearts also break. They need our love, encouragement and support, whilst they seek that place of forgiveness, restoration and healing.

As well as losing a ministry, some folk are wounded because the important hopes, which they had held for the future, or a vision to which they had been committed for a number of months or years, has not come to pass and does not seem likely to either. It can leave them with a deep sense of desolation and depression.

Chapter 2

Roots of Brokenness – Painful Relationships

Relationships – Affliction and Adversity

Any misfortune, affliction or calamity can also cause deep emotional pain, especially if it is repeated over and over again, as happened to Naomi. You may remember that her husband Elimelech and her two sons, Mahlon and Chilion, all died within the space of around ten years. They were living in the country of Moab at the time, and no doubt Naomi was feeling very angry, lost, sad and grief-stricken at what had happened to her and her family. Her response to her neighbours' glad cries of welcome as she returned home to Bethlehem was:

> *'Do not call me Naomi; call me Mara, for the Almighty has dealt very bitterly with me.'*   (Ruth 1:20)

'Naomi' meant pleasant and 'Mara' meant bitter, and that is just how a heartbroken person may feel: very bitter, angry and frustrated at the blows which life has dealt them.

Job was in a similar position; he had lost family members, servants, livestock, possessions, and his own health. Finally he cried out in his pain, anger and frustration, and he:

> *'Opened his mouth and cursed the day of his birth.'*

(Job 3:1)

We prayed with a man, many years ago now, who was in the same terrible and soul-destroying position as Job. He had lost his job, his family, and his health. One terrible blow after another, which not only crushed his body but also his heart. The most difficult thing for him to deal with, was his lack of understanding as to what was happening and where God was in the midst of it. I wonder if you have ever been there? Job was. It can be a very confusing position to be in and to be told, in the midst of it, that it is probably your own fault, will only add to the pain. If you have been there you will understand how Job felt at the advice of his 'so-called' friends.

Relationships – Unrequited Love

Strained or broken relationships may also contribute to the shattering or fracturing of the heart as sometimes happens in the case of someone experiencing **unrequited love**. There is a deep, twisting, and knife-like pain in loving another person, only to find that the love is not reciprocated. For example, unrequited love between single people, between a pastor and his congregation, or even between husband and wife.

In fact it is very difficult to continue to love someone who does not love you in return, and this may add to the pain, especially if you are expected to love him or her. This is certainly true as regards parents continuing to love their children who are in rebellion. It is even harder if the person actually hates or dislikes you intensely, as can happen in a number of different situations. We have only to consider the story of Jacob and Leah to see the depth of the pain felt by one spouse, when another rejects them.

> *'Then Jacob also went in to Rachel, and he also loved Rachel more than Leah.'* (Genesis 29:30)

It is interesting to see the Lord's response to Leah being unloved by her husband:

> *'When the Lord saw that Leah was unloved, He opened her womb; but Rachel was barren.'* (Genesis 29:31)

However when you consider the names which Leah gave to their children and see what they mean in Hebrew, you will begin to understand some of the devastation of unrequited love. Her firstborn she called Reuben, for she said:

> *'The Lord has surely looked on my affliction. Now therefore, my husband will love me.'* (Genesis 29:32)

She called her second son, Simeon,

> *'Because the Lord has heard that I am unloved, He has therefore given me this son also.'* (Genesis 29:33)

Her third son she called Levi, convincing herself that,

> *'Now this time my husband will become attached to me, because I have borne him three sons.'* (Genesis 29:34)

And her fourth son she called Judah, declaring that now she would:

> *'Praise the Lord.'* (Genesis 29:35)

One gets the impression that Leah has eventually won through to a place of contentment either with or without her husband's help. Certainly we see that the Lord had a heart for her in the midst of her pain and her loveless marriage.

Relationships – Betrayal

In this area of painful relationships, betrayal of one another goes very deep. It may be that, as in the case of the disciple Peter, it is our betrayal of others, which causes the breaking of our hearts:

> *'And Peter remembered the word of Jesus word of Jesus who had said to him, "Before the rooster crows, you will deny me three times." Then he went out and wept bitterly.'*
> (Matthew 26:27)

Conversely it may be that **others** have betrayed us. Such betrayal strikes at the very centre of our being, especially if it happens, as it did in the case of Hazel, whose husband betrayed her by going off with her best friend. 'The greatest pain,' she said, 'Was that it was my trusted friend who was involved, it seemed like a double betrayal.' Fellow-workers can also cause each other deep pain through an act of betrayal; there is also the trust that is betrayed by a well-loved leader: maybe his congregation believed the best, but received the worst. Sometimes the leader has his congregation stolen away from him, as happened in the case of a minister whose elder took half the congregation with him to start a new fellowship, causing deep wounding and fractured trust that is still in the process of being healed today.

Chapter 3

Roots of Brokenness – Abuse, Sin and Trauma

Abuse

Any form of abuse whether it is physical, spiritual, verbal, emotional or sexual, will cause a deep wounding in the heart, and really requires a book in itself! Sexual abuse in particular goes very, very deep indeed and as well as breaking the heart, it also I believe, has the potential of breaking the human spirit. Truly it can be said of such people that:

> *'By sorrow of the heart the spirit is broken.'*

(Proverbs 15:13)

The sexual act is not just a physical activity but it involves the whole person, so if the sexual act becomes abusive, the whole person will suffer the consequences: their spirit, soul and body will be deeply pained and hurt in one way or another.

Scripture is full of stories of **sexual abuse**, which I find very encouraging, in that it tells us that this is not a new phenomena which surprises our heavenly Father, but rather an old problem which He is well able to meet. The story of Tamar and Amnon is a very well known example and records the incestuous story of how Tamar, a beautiful young girl, was sexually abused by her half-brother Amnon. (As a matter of interest, it is very interesting to trace the family history of Amnon through his father King David. We discover in his ancestry the person of Judah, who was the son of Jacob and Leah. Judah had an ungodly incestuous, relationship with his daughter-in-law, also named Tamar (Genesis 38), the result of which was the birth of twin boys. One of the boys was named 'Perez', who is a direct ancestor of Amnon. There are ten generations between Perez and Amnon, reminding us that for sexual sin, ten generations may suffer the sins of the fathers (Deuteronomy 23:2).

Tamar had gone into her brother's bedroom, a virgin, completely innocent and free, but after the abuse she came out full of shame, guilt, fear and a broken heart. It completely devastated her and Scripture records that:

> *'Tamar dwelt in her brother Absalom's house, a desolate woman.'* (2 Samuel 13:20)

In the dictionary 'desolation' means 'solitary, uninhabited, neglected, barren, forlorn, wretched'. It could have added 'heartbroken', for that is how many sexually abused people feel; at the moment of abuse their heart is figuratively if not actually broken. Because the person who has abused them is often a well-loved figure – father, uncle, mother, brother – the heart of the abused person is open towards them, so when the person is taken advantage of sexually, the heart that was previously given in love, now becomes divided and broken. There is often within their being, a mixture of love and hatred, and a blend of ambivalent feelings.

Verbal abuse is also a very powerful weapon against another, especially in the hands of a family member, a friend, an authority figure or a deeply beloved person. As the writer of Proverbs records:

> *'Death and life are in the power of the tongue.'*
> (Proverbs 18:21)

And certainly we can see that this is so in the case of Hannah and Peninnah, as recorded in 1 Samuel, chapter 1. Peninnah was the wife of Elkanah as also was Hannah. Peninnah had children, whilst Hannah had none and every day Peninnah fed 'daily death' into Hannah's spirit.

> *'So it was, year by year, when she went up to the house of the Lord, that she* [Peninnah] *provoked her; therefore she* [Hannah] *wept and did not eat.'* (1 Samuel 1:7)

Any verbal words of abuse, especially if spoken by key people in your life, can cause brokenness on the inside. 'You're ugly.' 'No one will ever want to marry you.' 'I hate you, you will never get close to me.' Or as someone shared with me quite recently, a very hurtful word that had been said against them: 'There is nothing about you which I like, nor will there ever be, so it doesn't matter what you say or do, you will never make me love you again.' Such words bring death to the spirit and brokenness of heart.

Spiritual abuse also causes great pain amongst the Body of Christ, and I believe, to the Lord Himself. He has said that He would deal with those who cause hurt and pain amongst His flock and that He Himself will:

> *'Search for My sheep and seek them out.'* (Ezekiel 34:11)

Promising to:

> *'Seek what was lost and bring back what was driven away, bind up the broken and strengthen what was sick.'*
> (Ezekiel 34:16)

However it is not only fellowships that are abused by their leadership, but also congregations that sometimes spiritually abuse their leaders. We have prayed with many pastors and pastor's wives, whose lives have been devastated and almost destroyed by the poisonous words and actions of some of their congregations. Because the leaders and the congregations human spirits are open towards one another, for the purpose of building one another up, and feeding life and strength into one another, there is also with this openness, the potential to break one another down; thus using the very means of good, which God has provided, in order to attack and destroy.

Physical abuse also goes very deep and often results in a battering on the inside as well as on the outside. The physical bruises which can be seen may elicit sympathy and help, but from whom do you receive compassion and assistance for a bruised and beaten heart? One of the most damaging kinds of physical abuse is that which occurs between spouse and spouse, because of the 'one flesh' relationship between them. Naturally, if there are any children, this compounds the problem, for it always involves them, as they will respond to the fear, tension and anxiety within the home. The care and protection of the children simply adds to the heartbreak of the one being abused, who tries to put on a brave face for 'the sake of the children'. Thus it becomes an added burden.

Sin

Sin always has a consequence in the life of a person, but in a Christian it has the capacity to break the heart if it is entered into wilfully. I remember the story of one man, who for forty years had suffered from deep depression, because he had committed adultery with a former girl-friend. Intercourse had only taken place once, and after that he had never seen the girl again, but the man was so deeply ashamed that he never told anyone of his sin, but instead he hid it away in his heart. The buried sin began to do its work, eventually to the point of breaking his heart. The consequences were disastrous within his marriage and his family. Not because they knew of his sin through confession, but because he was walking around with a broken and despairing heart. This is most likely to happen if the person is normally a man after God's own heart, as was King David.

After his adulterous sin with Bathsheba and his deep repentance he cries out:

> *'A broken and a contrite heart (broken down with sorrow for sin and humbly and thoroughly penitent), such, O God, You will not despise.'*   (Psalm 51:17, Amplified Bible)

And of course the Lord did not condemn David, He forgave

and re-instated him, but not without repercussions within his own life and the life of his family.

However, it is not only our own sin, but also the sin which others perpetuate against us, which can also be heart rending. This can be especially true concerning the sins of our children, when we have endeavoured to bring them up in the 'nurture of the Lord'. Jane was such a child. She went through Sunday school, was taught by her parents the Christian values of the family and was set a good example by her mother and father. During her teenage years she got involved with a group at school who were dabbling in drugs and started to experiment herself. The outcome was that she ended up a broken young woman and her parents lived the rest of their lives (until they received some prayer) with shattered dreams and broken hearts. The continual questioning: 'What could we have done differently?' 'Where did we go wrong?' 'Should we have read the signs earlier?' etc., only added to their heartache.

Trauma

Any kind of trauma, at each stage of our lives has the potential of having an inward as well as an outward effect. Traumas, even whilst in the womb, can be devastating and life changing, like the lady whose mother fell down the stairs whilst she was six months pregnant with her. This caused the child to suffer from great fears and phobias throughout her young life, which caused immense repercussions in the relationships which she tried to form later on. She continually found that a paralysing fear and a lack of trust always got in the way. She was eventually healed when she became a Christian and spent much time in prayer and fellowship, over a number of months, with loving Christian friends. Many folk are walking around after a traumatic accident with only partial healing. They may have received physical healing but they still carry around the heavy burden of an unhealed heart within; a heart which had been broken by fear, anxiety or the loss of others at the time of the accident.

Chapter 4

Roots of Brokenness – Abandonment, Loneliness and Rejection

Abandonment

Some people are abandoned very early on in life, through no fault of their own, and yet they feel compelled to continually spend a lot of time seeking the reasons for that abandonment. One lady, who with her twin sister had been left as babies in a telephone box by their mother who couldn't cope, wrote:

> 'Throughout my life, I was constantly searching for my mother, for the woman who had given me life. Even though we had wonderful foster parents, I felt that if only I could find her, I would discover the reasons for her leaving us as she did. The fact that she had left a note stating what those reasons were, didn't satisfy my heart, I needed to hear them from her. My wedding day and the day on which my own babies were born were the hardest.'

A sense of abandonment can also take root in the heart of a child when parents are divorced, or separated, for a child will often feel responsible and guilty for the break-up of the marriage even though, to an adult, this would be totally unreasonable. The guilt somehow seems to seal in the fact that they 'deserved' to be left and abandoned. This can also happen if a mother or father dies whilst the child is quite young. Because a child hasn't developed the reasoning abilities of an adult, they will very often lay the blame for the divorce or the death at their own door, and reckon that in that case they deserved to be abandoned. As well as wounding of the emotions you will often find, in such a situation, a person has a very low self-image.

Loneliness

Loneliness and rejection can spring from a number of different causes, which we are not able to consider in much depth in this book, but nevertheless they are kindred feelings and often walk hand in hand. Many people, in differing circumstances, and for different reasons, feel the stress of loneliness. For example, the loneliness of an incomplete and loveless marriage, or the single person feeling less than whole unless married. Both know the aching loneliness of always seeming to be the one going to places alone or being with a spouse and yet not really walking in companionship. There is the grief-stricken loneliness of bereavement, of constantly looking at an empty chair; the single parent with only children for company; or the teenager feeling isolated within the peer group. Sometimes older people, who feel useless and unwanted, experience the intense loneliness of waiting for death.

Loneliness can be solely a physical phenomenon, or it can be a sickness in the spirit. It can even be forced upon us by circumstances, or slipped into by not taking the due care necessary to nurture the family and the friendships which we already have. Certain people find church to be a very lonely place indeed, especially if they don't fit into the natural groupings that are available, such as the young wives meeting, mums and toddlers groups, youth gatherings or women's meetings.

As we have already stated loneliness and rejection are

common bedfellows and most people will have suffered from the effects of both at some time or other in their lives. Rejection has the grave potential of breaking the heart. The reality of **rejection** was common even to Jesus, for He truly was a rejected man, suffering alienation at many people's hands and at varying times throughout His life. King Herod rejected Him shortly after His birth and He was set aside continually by His own people. It was as St John records:

'He came to His own and His own did not receive Him.'
(John 1:11)

Even His earthly family, His hometown, His leaders, His disciples, and it seemed His Father (at the Cross) turned away from Him, causing Him to cry out in agony:

'My God, My God, why have You forsaken me?'
(Mark 15:34)

Yet having gone through all of that rejection Jesus sustained no lingering wounds, no bitterness filled His soul or poured out from His lips. Having been deeply rejected, He nevertheless chose not to pour out that rejection on others but rather to absorb it and walk in constant forgiveness of the perpetrators.

The Bible is full of illustrations concerning the different ways in which we can be rejected. For example, in Matthew 27:3–5 we read of the disciple, Judas, **rejecting himself** because of his deep remorse at his actions against Jesus. He cries out in Matthew 27:4:

'I have sinned by betraying innocent blood.'

In Luke 19:1–10 we see how Zaccheus was **rejected by society** and then we read in John 4:7–26 of the woman at the well being **rejected by many partners** as well as being rejected by the women of the village. There is the **rejection by the church** of the woman who sinned through adultery in John 8:1–11. As has been stated, everyone experiences some rejection throughout their lives, but how we respond to it will determine the extent of the devastation and whether we are broken by it or not.

Roots of Rejection

Rejection can take root right at the very moment of conception and this will be especially true if the baby has been conceived in anger or through rape. The womb is a very sensitive place and it is now widely realised that babies within the womb can sense and experience a whole lot more, emotionally and spiritually, than was at one time realised. For example, if one of the parents is deeply disappointed at the news of the pregnancy and speaks words of anger, pain and rejection in the presence of the child in the womb, this can give rise to a root of rejection, which may follow the child throughout its life. Words such as: 'I don't want another child,' 'This child is a serious mistake,' 'I intend to get rid of this baby.' If abortion is attempted, the effects of rejection will go even deeper, and some folks spend their lives trying to make up to parents, family or society for the fact that they survived the words of rejection or the attempted abortion. If you dig ever so shallowly, you will often find a wounded or a broken heart in such people.

The moment of birth is also a key time of acceptance or rejection. I am reminded of a very 'gentle' man who hid his gentleness for years because of his fear of rejection. His maternal grandmother had wanted a girl and had bought lots of pink dresses and bonnets for the new baby. She had waited a long time for a granddaughter and was eagerly looking forward to the event. When the baby was born, and it turned out to be a boy, so great was her frustration and anger that there was no way she was going to waste the pink clothes she had bought for the new arrival! So the little lad was dressed in pink clothes until he was nearly two. Everyone leaning over the pram exclaimed on what a lovely girl he was! He grew up hating anything 'girlish' and thus put aside his gentle nature in preference for the 'macho' image. For many years he lived a lie, denying his very nature, the untruth springing out of the rejection by his grandmother of his male gender. Alongside the rejection of his manhood, was a hardened heart, beneath which beat a grieving heart at the loss of his true nature.

We have looked at the way the loss of any relationship can break the heart and usually in such a situation, deep rejection will be involved and it will add to the shattering of the person involved. The breaking up of a marriage, the dissolving of a church or even the painful severing of a deep friendship which has gone wrong, with all the resulting pain of rejection, can and usually does, cause devastation and brokenness on the inside.

Results of Rejection

There appears to be a number of ways in which we, as human beings, handle rejection. The two most common methods are that we can either become very passive and as such learn to be 'people pleasers', or conversely we can become very angry and rebellious. Sometimes these reactions are described as that of **fight** or **flight**. When we fight the rejection the following lifestyle is uppermost.

Fight

We become very rebellious/argumentative/fiercely independent or even develop a very critical spirit. Anger, hostility, social aggression, and violence may be the way in which we react to any possible threat of future rejection. We may make a conscious or unconscious decision that we will dominate or manipulate others, and never again let anyone be in a position to push us around and therefore have the chance to hurt us again. This can result in a distorted image of God, ourselves and other people. It is almost as though we begin to expect rejection and our very reaction of rebelliousness brings that rejection about.

On the other hand, when we run away from rejection and the people who reject us, our lifestyle may be as follows:

Flight

We develop a deep fear of being constantly rejected by others, even to the point of making sure that we reject them first. Sometimes a crippling sense of inadequacy or shyness will grow within us and there will develop a need to withdraw or hide from people. Consequently we run from, avoid and even develop a fear of others. The fear being, of course, that if they really knew us they would not like us and therefore would reject us. So it is far easier and safer to reject them first! This hiding away may not only be from people, but also we may keep out of sight through our work; thus becoming a 'workaholic'. It may be that we make sure that we perform to a very high standard, consequently allowing performance orientation to take over and thus hide behind our 'image'. Sometimes there will grow within the person, who has been deeply rejected, a deep sense of injustice against every unfair cause, based of course, on the injustice of the prime rejection shown to oneself. Alongside the above there is usually an avoidance of any conflict situations, for conflict may bring rejection.

Within a rejected person there will probably be bred a deep lack of self-worth, a feeling of low self-esteem, an eroding of their confidence and a tremendous fear of intimacy. There may also be a feeling of guilt, deep loneliness and an obvious desire of trying too hard to please.

Unresolved Deep Emotional Pain

As we have seen, all of the above situations will leave a residue of pain and if this is left unresolved, then the pain itself will have the capacity to press down and contribute to a broken heart. The kinds of emotions, which you will find in the heart of the broken, are many and varied, depending on the reason or the root of the wounding. Often they will include the following feelings: a crippling sense of shame, the acute pain of grief, a constant lingering anxiety, the continual awareness of knowing humiliation, self-blame or the bitterness of blaming others. Sometimes a paralysing fear, angry resentment and depression will also take root.

Chapter 5

Reactions to Brokenness – Survival Strategies

Because we are spirit, soul and body whatever happens in one area of our lives will have repercussions in the other areas and certain reactions will follow. The following are some of the responses which we have seen throughout the years, as we have prayed for and ministered into broken lives. The most common and recognisable reactions are the **physical ones**. Sleeplessness is quite usual and the majority of people who are broken on the inside, will toss and turn for most of the night, only to fall fast asleep around five in the morning. Bad dreams or nightmares will often disturb their sleep, and if the pain is really deep these may include horrific flashbacks of past pain. It is also possible for a good number of infirmities to be evident in the life of the broken-hearted; stomach-ache or nervous stomach; migraines; backache as well as indeterminate aches and pains. Because the emotions are unexpressed in a healthy way, they will often find their own method of showing themselves through physical pain in the body. For some there may even be the physical reaction of using self-destructive tendencies, i.e. slashing oneself, picking infected sores on the body as well as the ultimate self-destructive action of suicide.

Then of course there are the **spiritual reactions**: according to the Scriptures:

'By sorrow of the heart the spirit is broken.'

(Proverbs 15:13)

So what takes place in the soul area, the mind the emotions and the will, will have an outworking within the human spirit. This is not the place to go into this area in depth, but for more information please see my book, *Healing the Human Spirit*. However it is important for us to realise that if we are receiving prayer, or praying for someone in this area of emotional wounding, then we will need to be aware that healing of the spirit will also be necessary. There will probably be a deep sadness in the person's spirit, as well as a lack of joy in the normal things in life. It may be that the emotional pain and wounding has gone so deep that a death wish will have taken root and suicide attempts may have taken place.

Volitional reactions, that is reactions within the will of the person, are also very likely. There may be a sense of indecisiveness about quite trivial decisions, a desire to manipulate others in order not to suffer further pain, or a deep rebellion against rules or authority figures. **Mental reactions** will probably include confused thinking, very anxious thought patterns which seem to go around in endless circles, and of course there will be certain **emotional reactions** which may take the form of fears, phobias and obsessions.

As we have noted, inside the heart of the broken you will undoubtedly find varying degrees of emotional pain: guilt, desolation, shame, grief, despair, anxiety, hopelessness, rejection, insecurity, loneliness, humiliation, blame, fear, resentment, and depression. God intended us to deal with our pain and hurt, in a godly way by finding right and helpful ways of expressing our deep inner feelings. If we don't, then we begin to learn to use certain **survival strategies** in order to cope with what seems to be an inescapable situation.

When we have been hurt deeply our first instinct is to hide away and nurse the pain, after which we eventually endeavour to deal with it as best we can. This is usually by expressing our feelings to the one who has wounded us, or by finding a safe outlet with some other person. If, however, we have learnt different patterns of dealing with our pain, for example by taking up the ostrich position and choosing not to deal with it or by running away from our pain, then more hurt and damage can ensue. The following are some of the strategies, which we may use in order to survive the pain, although in the end they will all tend to play us false!

Survival Strategies – Denial of Pain

One of the easiest ways to keep going through intense times of stress, pain and grief, is simply to deny that there is any problem at all. We maintain that we are doing fine; there is no problem! Really, we insist, there is no problem. Even though to everyone else concerned there obviously is a problem and a very large one at that. The observer, in this case, appears to see more of the action. The individual, who slips into a denial of pain, soon finds that it becomes a very convenient habit to develop. It is like slipping into a cupboard and staying out of sight, if anyone comes around that you don't like. Or putting your head under the blanket as a child and pretending that the bogey man will go away. Or, as a friend of mine used to do, sing as loud as she could, if I was saying something to her which she didn't want to hear. That's denial.

Linked in with this denial aspect is the whole area of **camouflaging** our pain, in that we put on a mask and pretend that everything is wonderful. We become the life and soul of the party, or we act out the clown or the independent observer. 'Yes there may be some pain,' we assert, 'but it has very little to do with us. We are over-comers!' Because we are in the denial mode we will do anything to mask the pain and not allow other people to see the real person behind the disguise. The 'super-spiritual' Christian fits in here too – the sugary sweet person, who never has an anxious moment, for whom there is never any pain, even though dreadful things might have happened to them. I am reminded of the lady who was divorced three times, and who had lost her only child in a car accident some six months before we met her. She insisted to us that, 'No she never felt any pain or ever needed to cry, even at the time of the death of her son.' There was a super-spiritual unreality about her. One felt that there was a deep unfathomable pool of tears within her that she had covered over with a sheet of ice. God gave us tears in order to grieve and release the pain, and it is true that no matter how much we mask the pain, it does not go away; it is simply covered over and left undealt with, with the capability of poking its head out whenever it likes. This is why we are sometimes taken by surprise by the intense feelings of sadness or fear we may experience at totally inappropriate moments. A girl I knew would often collapse into floods of tears, just when she wanted to be strong and brave. Her inner cupboard of pain had opened up and refused to be denied any longer. In a like manner one felt that sooner or later this sheet of ice would crack and the water would flow.

The sort of person we become, if we continue in this pattern of dealing with our pain, means that very soon we will begin to move into the realm of **unreality**. Out of our deep needs and fear, we refuse to allow other people to touch the **real** us. We develop the 'stiff upper lip' mentality and no matter what happens, no one, and in some instances this will also include the Lord, will be allowed to get too close to the inner part of our being. Thus we eventually develop a **deceptive heart** (which is sinful and needs to come to repentance). This deceptive heart covers over our broken heart which needs exposing in order to come to deep healing.

Dissection

In spite of the pain involved, some of us are so fascinated with our wounds, that we become like the little boy who is always digging up his apple seed to see if it has grown at all.

Or like the little girl who insists on removing the plaster to inspect the wound with an almost morbid fascination. Unfortunately all it does is to expose the seed and the wound to the air and hinder any possible growth or healing at all. It is the same with our pain. The more we look at it, **dissect** it or inspect it, the less likely it is that we will arrive at the place of dealing with our pain and allow it to come to a place of healing. Thus it may be used as a delaying tactic, because we feel that to deal with the pain would be too awful. It is possible, therefore, to continually look at the pain, and thus develop a **self-pitying heart** (again this is a sinful condition, which needs to come to repentance). In this state we learn to live with the 'Poor Old Me' syndrome. Our focus is always on ourselves; we feel that no one has, or ever will be able to understand or bring healing to the deep hurt within.

Drown the Pain

For some of us it is easier to drown the pain than to deal with it at the time and we may use many and varied ways of doing so. For example, one woman spent a great deal of her time escaping from pain by endlessly drowning it through the game of bridge. She played not just one, two or three after-noons a week, but every moment which was available was given over to the game. She would ring friends to arrange bridge party sessions morning, afternoon and evening, if at all possible. She was drowning her pain. For this lady it was to escape from the hurt of loneliness after a particularly nasty divorce.

We can use any of our hobbies to the same effect. Golf, swimming, football, tennis, knitting, or whatever leisure activity we may enjoy, can become obsessive and used as a drowning mechanism. That, which in itself may be good, can become a means of escape from the wholeness and healing which God desires us to enter into. The drowning may be by immersing yourself in any activity to excess, or simply by slumping in front of the television set, day after day and night after night.

Some of the most common 'drowning' activities are food, shopping, sport, drink, and work. I often wonder if the 'woman at the well' in St John's gospel was drowning her pain through sexual activity and that when Jesus said to her, *'You have had five husbands'* (John 4:18), He was actually pointing out to her that He was aware that she was lonely, rejected, sad and drowning her pain, as she tried to find acceptance and belonging through these many relationships. Certainly many folk who have been sexually abused say that they get into promiscuity because of a need to be accepted, but also in order to drown the pain of the abusive situations in which they have found themselves. Their attitude appears to be: 'Maybe this time it will be different and this relationship will ease the horrific memories which keep appearing like horror movies out of the dark.'

A fairly common escape method for the Christian is that of immersing oneself in church meetings, prayer meetings, Bible studies, etc., which at least would appear to have the spiritual value of getting you closer to God. However whilst that may be true in theory, in practice, very often the opposite happens. As we distance ourselves from people through these escape methods, no matter what form they may take, we also distance ourselves from God. If it is a father or mother doing this, it means that not only is the pain undealt with, but also the family misses out on the relationship input from mum or dad. This family time can be so sorely missed that it can turn a child or a spouse away from the things of God.

The person who has a tendency to drown their pain will also have the potential of becoming a very **restless** kind of person; the kind of human being who will always be on the run, always busy, never at rest or at peace. Interestingly, though, such folk long for the very peace from which they run away. They dare not stop long enough to wait for that peace to settle in their hearts, in case the hurt also catches up with them. Thus they develop a **restless heart** which runs away from looking at the brokenness within.

Burying the Pain

One of the ways of dealing, or not dealing, with painful emotions, is that of burying them and covering them over with a layer of concrete. Through the months and years of continuing pain, more concrete is added until there is layer upon layer upon layer, which it would take a strong explosive to break through. Unlike the 'denial' pattern, the person who buries the pain knows that there is pain there, but simply refuses to deal with it. Absalom, the son of King David, suggested to his younger sister Tamar (who had just been raped by her half-brother Amnon), that she indeed do just that!

> *'Do not take this thing to heart.'* (2 Samuel 13:20)

In other words, 'bury the pain,' he cautioned her strongly. Cover it over and get on with your life. Tamar took heed of her brother's words and unfortunately the outcome was what it often is in such an incident – deep desolation. We read that:

> *'Tamar remained desolate in her brother Absalom's house.'*
> (2 Samuel 13:20)

Truly this is a picture of someone who constantly buries his or her own heartache. There will develop in such a person a 'grit your teeth' mentality, a necessity to 'grin and bear it', however the proverbial weed of couch grass keeps popping up! And much time and effort will be spent trying to keep the emotions under control. There may be a tendency to become a **hard and inflexible** kind of person, someone with an **unyielding heart** that is gradually beginning to harden into the next condition, which really is very serious indeed.

Chapter 6

Reactions to Brokenness –
Defending the Pain

Defending the Pain

Some folks develop a way of putting a massive defence system around their pain, and whenever anyone approaches it they will use these defence mechanisms to keep him or her away. These defence systems are usually practised to perfection, but in the beginning they were formed out of a genuine need to protect their heartache. They were a means of preservation and survival. The trouble is that as they become more and more developed, they not only keep other people away from the pain, they keep God out as well. Such folk have a large 'No trespassers' notice right over their heart.

I call this 'The Secret Garden' syndrome. Those of you who have seen the film will know what I mean. A couple, very much in love, have a beautiful walled garden which the young wife tends lovingly and in which they and their child spend a great deal of time together. When the wife dies in the garden, through tragic circumstances, the husband, in deep pain, grief and anger, locks the door of the walled garden and throws away the key. No one at all is allowed into the garden; even his child is banned from playing in it. He defends the garden (and thus his pain) and protects it as best he can. (You will need to read the story to find out how this man's heart is healed!)

Self-defence

There are various methods, which can be used in order to defend the pain within the heart. We can, for example, use the tongue as a self-defence weapon. It is as good as a sword or a rapier to keep someone at bay, and as sharp as any genuine weaponry. The sarcastic reply to a genuine inquiry as to how a person feels will very quickly turn away sympathy or concern. The invective answer, full of poison when someone was being genuine and caring, will keep the 'well-intentioned' at bay. The attitude, 'I will attack you, before you attack me,' is an example of another well-used and skilled self-defensive tactic.

Brooding or sulking, is another self-defence strategy. 'If you do or say something that I don't like, that activates my pain. I do not like my pain touched and if you don't back off, then I will make you suffer for it. I will make sure that you don't do it again!' One woman would sulk for days at a time, and it came as no surprise to find that her husband soon learnt to creep around her and do everything in his power to keep the peace.

Self-destruct

Self-destructive tactics can work just as well as the self-defence ones. The attitude being that, 'I will put myself down first, before you do, because that will at least stop you from adding to my pain.' This is a fairly common ruse, especially in those who are struggling with low self-esteem and rejection. One person known to me personally used to dig her finger nails into her palms, in order not to feel her pain, or the grief and sadness of others. It works on the principle that it is better to hurt myself, rather than let others near to me and give them the potential to add to my wounds.

The Drawbridge Mentality

One way of protecting the pain is to use the drawbridge mentality, which is simply a pulling up of the drawbridge when friends, as well as enemies, approach and try to touch the real person. This may be an inner emotional or a spiritual withdrawal, which results in a distinct coldness in their manner, a feeling that they are there, yet not there. Some people actually withdraw physically when anyone is getting too close. They will go into the study and ignore everyone, or slam out of the house and go for a long walk that takes most of the day, whilst the rest of the family are left wondering, 'What have we done this time?'

Land Mines

The planting of land mines is a very effective, if immoral, defensive tactic, and can be as lethal as the land mines planted for physical destruction. The mines can be used both physically and emotionally. We plant them around the walls of our pain and if anyone comes too close, we blow a mine and frighten them off. It works on the principle that they will only do it once or twice and then they will learn that it is wise never to come too close again!

Anger is one of the land mines that can be used, and one that can be very potent indeed. Explosive anger which is very often linked to the original pain, but which has been added to over the years, would be activated as soon as someone tries to creep too close to them. For example, there is the woman whose husband knows better than to mention his wife's family, because of the anger that that will trigger off. This is often called pressing a 'hot button'.

If we continue in these patterns of behaviour we will inevitably become a very **defensive** kind of person, and a callus will develop around our heart, which over time, will turn into a **stony heart**. In Scripture this is a very serious condition indeed, and our last state therefore becomes worse than the first, for now we find that we have a broken heart, being protected and covered over by a stony heart.

Thus we have seen that it depends very much on how we deal with our pain as to what kind of heart we develop before God and other people. To sum up: if we **deal** with our pain as the Lord intended, this will result in us developing a **compassionate heart** towards others, for we will have allowed our own pain to soften our heart and reach out in sympathy towards other people in similar circumstances. However if we **disown and deny** the pain, this will cause us to develop a **deceptive heart** which will have repercussions in every other area of our lives. If we constantly **dissect** the pain, a **selfish heart** will be the result and it may be that we are totally unaware of the pain of other people. Conversely, if we use some of the above mentioned methods to **drown** the pain, we may become very nervous, anxious people who are always rushing around and running away from those things which threaten to hurt us. Thus we will develop a **restless heart**. If we continually **bury** our pain, our heart will become hard and unyielding, whilst if we choose to **defend** the pain, the unfortunate result will be the development of a **stony heart**.

Chapter 7

The Stony Heart

Scripture gives many instances of those whose hearts have become hard and stony. For example, in 2 Chronicles 36:13 we see the rebelliousness and the hardness of Zedekiah's heart. He was twenty-one years old when he came to the throne and he reigned for eleven years in Jerusalem. We are told that he did evil in the sight of the Lord and would take no notice of the warnings of Jeremiah the prophet, as recorded in Jeremiah 21. Thus through sin, he developed a heart of stone and we read:

> *'He stiffened his neck and hardened his heart against turning to the Lord God of Israel.'* (2 Chronicles 36:13)

It could also be said, of course, that King David developed a heart of stone because of his sin with Bathsheba. In fact we can see a gradual progression of the hardening of his heart as he gets deeper and deeper into sin. After his adultery with Bathsheba, he moves into deception as he brings husband, Uriah the Hittite, home from war, hoping that people will think that the baby which Bathsheba is carrying will be taken for Uriah's and not for his. A further hardening takes place as he writes a letter to Joab, a commander in David's army, and brutally orders the death of Bathsheba's husband, Uriah the Hittite:

> *'And he wrote in the letter, saying, "Set Uriah in the forefront*
> *of the hottest battle, and retreat from him, that he may be*
> *struck down and die."'* (2 Samuel 11:15)

When God sent the prophet Nathan to challenge David about his sin, it is interesting to note that his response to his wrongdoing was totally different from Zedekiah's reaction:

> *'Then David said to Nathan, "I have sinned against the*
> *Lord."'* (2 Samuel 12:13)

And later in the book of Psalms we see him crying out to God to break his hard, stony and rebellious heart. He groans:

> *'Have mercy upon me, O God,*
> *According to Your lovingkindness;*
> *According to the multitude of Your tender mercies,*
> *Blot out my transgressions.'* (Psalm 51:1)

He goes on to cry:

> *'Create in me a clean heart, O God,*
> *And renew a steadfast spirit within me.'* (Psalm 51:10)

In Ezekiel God says about Israel's heart that:

> *'The house of Israel will not listen to you, because they will*
> *not listen to me; for all the house of Israel are impudent and*
> *hardhearted.'* (Ezekiel 3:7)

It was also said of King Nebuchadnezzar that:

> *'His heart was lifted up, and his spirit was hardened in pride,*
> *he was deposed from his kingly throne, and they took his glory*
> *from him.'* (Daniel 5:20)

It is interesting to note that Scripture records here that what happens in the heart has the possibility of hardening the spirit also.

A **stony heart** is similar to having a callus on a wound, underneath which the pain and the infection of the heart-ache continue to fester, thus providing ideal ground for the growth of many and varied **bitter shoots**. These bitter shoots are certain attitudes, which we hold against other people who have hurt us; or maybe which we hold against God or sometimes ourselves. These attitudes will eventually, if left to grow, produce a **sinful heart**, which then goes on to bring forth bitter **fruits** of sinful **behaviour patterns**.

We find therefore that **legitimate pain**, if allowed to harden, will turn into **sinful attitudes**, which will then start to form within us a **sinful heart**. Out of this sinful heart will flow **fruits** of **sinful behaviour**. The following are some of the legitimate painful emotions, which if allowed to fester and grow within the **stony heart**, will result in a lifestyle of sinful attitudes and behaviour patterns.

Shame is a normal emotion, which we may experience as a result of being betrayed or let down. However if it is not expressed and dealt with in a godly way it may gradually harden into a critical attitude: 'Well I'm not so bad, what about them?' We eventually end up by attacking others in order to defend our own shame. We begin the pattern of behaviour of putting others down in order to hide our own humiliation.

In the whole area of grief, which is a natural process to walk through, there is the potential of becoming twisted and the genuine emotion turns, as with Mara, into an attitude of bitterness. This, in itself will develop into a pattern of expectation. 'Oh nothing good ever happens to me, I always seem to get hit.' 'If something bad is going to happen, it'll be to me!' 'Everyone is against me, even God.'

Anxiety, if pushed down and hardened, may ultimately turn into withdrawal and result in a behavioural pattern of sulking and avoidance of people. 'I'm too fearful of facing you and the future, therefore I will dwell on my fears and withdraw into my safety zone.' Rejection, as we have seen, is a big area of pain and if it is pushed down and not dealt with, will eventually harden into rebellion, which may result in a lifestyle of drugs, promiscuity and hitting out at all authority figures. The fruit of this is 'attack is the best form of defence,' and 'I'll hit you before you hit me first.' If a person has suffered from humiliation, very often it will turn into a perverted form of pride, the outcome of which, is 'I will never let anyone humiliate me in that way again.' This may be linked in with the emotion of shame. A fierce independence begins to take root.

If someone has been blamed for something of which they were not guilty, or if they blame themselves for something of which they feel guilty, and they refuse to release the emotion in a godly way then it can harden into revenge. 'You did this to me, and I intend to get my own back,' or as someone once said: 'I will see my way with you, you'll not be allowed to blame me again.' Before long a vindictive life-style can take root. The genuine emotion of fear may harden into suspicion, and as one man who had been badly hurt and feared further pain, said: 'I've come to the realisation that you can't trust anyone, everyone wants something from you, everyone will eventually let you down.'

Resentment is a really difficult emotion to deal with, but unless we do so it will have the potential of hardening into a feeling of hatred, especially against the person responsible for the pain. That resentment will then bring forth the fruit of volcanic reactions. There will be a 'blowing of the top' whenever something seems 'unjust,' or 'unfair'. This is a replay of the original 'unjust' position in which the person found himself or herself.

Depression is often found in the heart of the wounded and if it is continually pushed down and ignored, either by others or the people concerned, it may turn into a death wish. There may grow an attitude within the person of 'What's the use? I might as well give up – I might as well be dead,' and suicide may be attempted. I have drawn a chart of a number of different legitimate emotions which may be found in the broken heart, and how these can harden into sinful attitudes and fruits of behaviour. There are, of course, other emotions, which we do not have the space to mention.

The Stony Heart

Legitimate pain ➤	Sinful attitude ➤	Sinful behaviour
(a) Shame	Criticism	Attack/form of defence
(b) Grief	Bitterness	'Expectation' syndrome
(c) Anxiety	Withdrawal	Sulking strategy
(d) Rejection	Rebellion	Drugs/alcohol abuse
(e) Humiliation	Pride	'Independent' factor
(f) Blame	Revenge	Vindictiveness
(g) Fear	Suspicion	Mistrust rules!
(h) Resentment	Hatred	Volcanic reactions
(i) Depression	Death wish	Attempted suicide

We need to learn how to bring our stony, sinful broken hearts to the Cross for breaking, cleansing and healing.

Chapter 8

The Place of the Cross

It is vitally important for those who are ministering into the emotionally wounded to remember that beneath a stony heart there is a broken heart, which needs healing. This will save us from becoming very judgmental and lecturing people for their sinful attitudes and behaviour. As we shall see later, these **will** need to be repented of, and turned away from, but we must always remember that the person underneath is in deep pain and to some extent will be locked into these sinful patterns of behaviour, until a measure of healing has taken place. We need to learn how to lead people to the Cross for healing and freedom, for it is in, and through Jesus, that the heartbroken are restored and made whole.

Jesus has a heart, which beats for the heartbroken. We see Him expressing that heart, which was finally broken on the Cross, as He moves around the area of Galilee, Nazareth and Jerusalem, bringing healing and wholeness to the desolate and distressed. For example, He befriends the alienated and the lonely. Matthew 8:1 tells the story of the man who had leprosy, a physical complaint but also with the pain of isolation and loneliness locked in. A man separated from his family, from his opportunity to work and from society in general.

In Luke 8:42–48 we are told about how a woman with an issue of blood is healed. She had been bleeding for twelve years and had tried many doctors, thus showing her determination and desperation. For those who know the Jewish laws, they will realise that when she touched Jesus, not only was her blood flow healed, but also the pain of her broken heart at not being able to touch and hug her family, just in case she made them 'unclean'. Zaccheus, when he was encouraged to come down out of the tree, was also brought out of the isolation, into which he had become locked because of his sin (Luke 19:1–9).

Jesus also healed people from guilt and condemnation, as the story of the woman taken in adultery illustrates. Those famous words in John 8:11:

> *'Neither do I condemn you; go and sin no more,'*

have been a means of blessing and release to many a guilty, heartbroken person ever since, as have the words spoken to that other sinful woman who anointed Jesus' feet in the house of Simon the Pharisee:

> *'Your sins are forgiven.'* (Luke 7:48)

Jesus moreover touched the heart of the woman at the well (John 4), ministering deep into her rejection issues with His love and acceptance, and He also dispelled disappointment and vain regrets from the hearts of the two on the road to Emmaus (Luke 24).

The act of betrayal by Peter was personally forgiven by Jesus and it is extraordinary to see how gently, but firmly, Jesus reinstates him, thus bringing healing to his bruised heart. Three times Peter had spoken betrayal, declaring that he never knew Jesus, had never met Him; three times Jesus affirms Peter's love and calling:

> *'Jesus said to Simon Peter, "Simon, son of Jonah, do you love Me more than these?" He said to Him, "Yes Lord; You know that I love You." He said to him, "Feed My lambs."'*
>
> (John 21:15)

Those who were heavy-hearted and weary were also encouraged to approach Jesus, and they have done so ever since. In Matthew 11:28 the call is unequivocal and clear:

47

> *'Come to Me, all you who labor and are heavy laden, and I will give you rest.'*

And, of course, the grief-stricken and distressed were never far away from Jesus' compassionate heart. We see this in His encounter with the widow of Nain, as He entreats her:

> *'Do not weep.'* (Luke 7:13)

Jesus then goes on to display His deep ability to suffer with people, as He proceeds to raise her only son from the dead. We find Him drawing alongside and comforting Mary in the garden after the resurrection (John 20:10–18), and also the grieving father when the man's daughter was at the point of death, encouraging him:

> *'Do not be afraid; only believe.'* (Mark 5:36)

Jesus, through His life, was simply demonstrating what would become widely available through His death on the Cross, for His life's work, which was finally accomplished by His death, was to **'heal the brokenhearted.'**

The compassionate heart which beat for others whilst He was alive, was finally broken on the Cross, in order that our hearts might be healed. Isaiah 53:4 reminds us that:

> *'He has borne our griefs*
> *And carried our sorrows.'*

It is there at the Cross, that the stones of sin are removed through confession and repentance. It is at the Cross, that our pain and suffering can be released onto Jesus, who came to heal the brokenhearted. It is at the Cross, that the healing love of Jesus is able to flow into our wounded and broken hearts.

It is important to see that something very deep was happening when Jesus died upon the Cross and took our sin upon Himself. For it was on the Cross that a godly transference took place, it was there that our **stony, sinful** hearts were transferred onto Jesus, and because of that transference we see that His heart was broken for us. John the disciple records that:

> *'One of the soldiers pierced His side with a spear, and immediately blood and water came out.'*   (John 19:34)

Blood and water denote a broken heart; thus symbolically showing forth that our stony hearts of sin and pain, broke His heart. Moreover as the blood and water flowed onto the ground at the foot of the Cross, I believe something very deep and profound was happening. There is a law in God's universe, which is called the law of 'sowing and reaping'. Galatians 6:7 tells us:

> *'Do not be deceived, God is not mocked; for whatever a man sows, that he will also reap.'*

On the Cross Jesus sowed a broken heart, a heart which was broken because of the weight of man's sin. His heart was **also** broken because of the weight of man's hurt, griefs, infirmities and pain. He knew betrayal: by Judas, Peter and all of His closest friends. They all ran and left Him. As Jesus hung upon the Cross He experienced deep rejection, both from His family and His dearest friends. He also suffered the agonies of walking the road of bleak loneliness for us, and going through the valley of the shadow of death and grief on our behalf. He experienced in a deeper way than any of us will ever experience, the struggle and the torment of knowing abandonment, even from His Father:

> *'My God, My God, why have You forsaken me?'*
> (Matthew 27:46)

More than that, as we bring our stony, sinful hearts to Him, the hardness of our stony hearts is broken, as we look on His deep and compassionate love for us, and thus He is able to confront, pierce and remove the stones of our sinful attitudes and behaviour. It is at the Cross and through the Cross that true confession and repentance take place. Nevertheless, it is important to realise that this is a process, which may take place over a period of time, but it is a process which He is committed to seeing us through. As He does so He gradually begins to reap that which He sowed on the Cross – even our 'broken hearts'.

More than that, after the stony heart is broken and the stones of sin are removed, we are then enabled to release the pain from our wounded hearts onto Jesus on the Cross, for as we have already stated, He came to carry our sorrows and griefs.

More than that, after we release our pain, grief, fear, guilt, shame and sorrow onto Him, He joyfully, through the Holy Spirit, releases His heart into us, and so fulfils the promise of the New Covenant:

> *'I will give you a new heart and put a new spirit within you; I will take the heart of stone out of your flesh and give you a heart of flesh.'*   (Ezekiel 36:26)

Thus His love, compassion, faithfulness, obedience, servant- and shepherd-heart flows into us with healing both for ourselves and through us into the lives of others. **Thus there is a godly exchange of heart attitudes and emotions**.

Chapter 9

Ministering to Emotional Wounds

The promise, as recorded in Ezekiel, is that God will remove our stony hearts and give us a heart of flesh. As we have seen, the manner in which He does this is through the Cross of the Lord Jesus Christ. Thus the Cross is all important, as the means whereby the stony heart is broken and the broken heart healed. Therefore for those people who are wounded in their emotions, they need to learn to move forward into their healing by the way of the Cross. They must face up to dealing with the sinful attitudes and behaviour patterns of which they have been guilty, through confession and repentance, and be willing for the stony concrete around their hearts to be removed. The painful feelings will need to be released to the Lord and as they give them to Him, they will begin to receive from the Lord the heart of flesh.

For ease of reference, for those who will be ministering to the heartbroken, I have listed the stages of release in note form. It is of course, always crucial to remember that it is the Holy Spirit who does the ministry and our total reliance is on Him and the gifts which He gives and uses through us, to bring people into that place of healing and freedom. It is also vital to remember that we always need to ask the Holy Spirit to reveal to us the **root** or the reason for the person's broken heart, for it may have been buried deep for a number of years. It is only when we get to the root or to the source of the pain that, like a good surgeon, we can expose it to the healing flow of the Holy Spirit.

Summary of How to Minister into Emotional Wounds

Stage 1: Discerning the root

1. Ask the Holy Spirit to reveal the root of the heartache, either through the person concerned or through a word of knowledge, or another of His gifts.
2. Wait patiently for Him to work. The person may begin to share a memory with you or you may receive a picture or a word, which opens up the root of the pain.

Stage 2: Removal of bitter shoots

1. **Confession and repentance**: The person will need to speak out their confession and repentance for any known sin which they have been into, especially as regards the pain within their hearts. They will need to confess any resentment, bitterness or anger that they have held towards another, as well as any sinful attitudes or behaviour patterns which they have walked in. Maybe they will need to speak out their repentance for using sinful survival strategies or ungodly ways of dealing with their pain and hurt as well.
2. **Forgiveness**: The person will need to choose to walk on the path of forgiveness all of the time; forgiveness towards others, in whatever way they may have hurt them; as well as choosing to forgive oneself wherever that is necessary.

   True forgiveness always includes the willingness for:
3. **Reconciliation**: There is a very moving story of reconciliation between Joseph and his brothers in the book of Genesis. Joseph had been very badly treated by his brothers, for they had isolated, rejected and abandoned

him. However, Joseph found it in his heart to forgive them and be reconciled to them. We read:

> *'Then Joseph said to his brothers, "I am Joseph; does my Father still live?" But his brothers could not answer him, for they were dismayed in his presence. And Joseph said to his brothers, "Please come near to me." And they came near. And he said: "I am Joseph your brother, whom you sold into Egypt. But now, do not therefore be grieved or angry with yourselves because you sold me here; for God sent me before you to preserve life." . . . Moreover he kissed all his brothers and wept over them, and after that his brothers talked with him.'* (Genesis 45:3–5, 15)

That is reconciliation.

Stage 3: Removal of concrete

1. There will need to be a further time of repentance for not dealing with our pain in the way in which God intended. A repentance for not expressing our emotions in a godly way and thus allowing our hearts to become hard and stony.
2. We will need to choose to become vulnerable, not only to God but also to other people.
3. We will also need to choose to allow the Holy Spirit to break that concrete wall down in His own time and way, and we will probably need to speak out our willingness to trust Him to open the cupboard doors and move into our pain.

Stage 4: Pain released

1. Ask the Lord to deal with each area of pain that has been hidden.
2. Ask the Lord to bring to the surface the memory related to that area of pain.
3. Ask the Lord to build a bridge between the memory and the area of pain.

4. Whilst waiting, in an expectant attitude of prayer for the Holy Spirit to work, the person will begin to experience again the original emotion which had been buried.

5. Get the person to speak out and acknowledge the feeling, for example: 'There is anger there, or fear, or sadness.'

6. Get the person to acknowledge the emotion as their own: 'I feel angry.' 'I feel frightened.' 'I feel sad.' They will probably begin to experience afresh the original emotion under the direction of the Holy Spirit.

7. The person will then need to give the pain, anger, fear, grief etc., to the Lord on the Cross. (It will again help if they speak it out.)

8. Help them to see, by faith, the godly transference of their sin and pain onto Jesus. This may take a long time and requires much patience on the part of the one who is ministering.

9. Be aware that the demonic may be present and, if so, will need addressing and casting out in the Name of Jesus.

10. Wait until one area of pain has been dealt with before proceeding to the next.

11. When you feel in your spirit that the pain, and any demonic if present, has been dealt with, ask the Holy Spirit to move you on to Stage 5.

Stage 5: Receive your healing

1. Pour godly nourishment and support into the area into which you have been ministering. What you pour in will all depend on the wounding and pain which has been released. For example, if you have been dealing with grief, bereavement and death, begin to feed **life** from the Cross into them. Speak into their spirits the truth that Jesus is the resurrection and the life. Feed all the benefits of the Cross into them. Take as much time, if necessary, to feed truth in as you took to release the pain and the wounding.

2. Begin to feed hope and comfort into them. Ask the Holy Spirit, the Comforter, to come and comfort their spirit. Ask Him to speak hope deep into their inner being; to find that part of them that is lonely, abandoned, etc., and raise expectancy deep within them that God is for them and is bringing them into healing.

3. Feed purpose and vision into them, just as God did with Elijah. Ask the Lord for a specific word of encouragement and direction for them.

4. Feed the Word of God into them. Ask the Lord for a *rhema* word for them – a word from Scripture that is directly applicable to their situation.

5. Be prepared to walk with the person until they come to the place of restoration.

Chapter 10

Restoration from Emotional Wounds

Although it is very important that the person who is emotionally wounded walks through the above ministry procedures, it is also essential to realise that for most people the long restoration process is also a key issue of walking into wholeness. Scripture is full of clues as to the ingredients which are essential for good nurturing to take place, in order that true and lasting restoration. becomes a reality.

For example, in the book of Ruth we find that **committed friendship** is a key to nurturing and restoration. We saw earlier that Naomi had lost her husband and both of her sons through death, in a relatively short space of time. Her daughter-in-law, Ruth, committed herself fully to Naomi, even though it was at quite a price, for it meant that she would have to leave her own family and country in order to support her mother-in-law. For someone who is walking through pain, grief and even bitterness of soul, as Naomi was, it is a priceless gift to have another person walk there with you; a person who is committed to you, no matter what happens. To offer such friendship is, as with Ruth, very costly but also very productive.

Ruth, of course, knew something of the 'well of pain' in her own experience, for she was recently widowed herself and no doubt missed her husband very much indeed. A friend who will see you through until you are fully restored, is one who has at least walked in the 'shadow' of the valley, if not in the full blast of the gale. Such people are enabled:

> *'To comfort those who are in trouble, with the comfort with which we ourselves are comforted by God.'*
>
> (2 Corinthians 1:4)

Because Ruth was familiar with the world of pain, she would be able to bring a depth of understanding and effective nurturing into her dealings with Naomi. Ruth, I believe, would feed encouragement, affirmation, love, a sense of worth and value into her mother-in-law, on a continuing basis, thus feeding and strengthening her spirit and aiding the restoration process. There was also a genuine kindliness about Ruth's friendship with her mother-in-law, which would be like a soothing balm to the troubled woman's soul:

> *'And Naomi said to her two daughters-in-law, "Go, return each to her mother's house. The Lord deal kindly with you, as you have dealt with the dead and with me." '* (Ruth 1:8)

However, there was no turning back for Ruth, for she was:

> *'Determined to go with her.'* (Ruth 8:18)

I remember the story of one young girl who came through to a tremendous place of healing, simply because two ladies within her church were, like Ruth, totally committed to seeing her through to health and wholeness. They were available to her every hour of the day and night. She was encouraged to phone them at any time, and often she would call their homes in the early hours of the morning, when she felt most fearful, and one or other of them would patiently take her call. Their homes were open to her; their families became her family; their church became her church. They nurtured her for weeks, months and even for a number of years. Without such **committed, but costly friendship** I am convinced she would not have come to the place of healing which she is in today.

Another ingredient for true restoration to take place, linked in with the above, is that of allowing all the **time** that is necessary for healing to come to fruition. We live in a **'now'** society, but God is never in a hurry and those who minister and stand alongside hurting people need to learn that God's timing is very often different from our own. In Genesis 37:34–35 we read of the deep grief of Jacob when he heard of the supposed death of his dearly beloved son, Joseph. Jacob in fact, was so grief-stricken that:

'He refused to be comforted, and he said, "For I shall go down into the grave to my son in mourning." Thus his father wept for him.'

Later we find that Jacob was still in deep mourning when his sons want to take Benjamin to Joseph in Egypt and Jacob cries out:

'My son shall not go down with you, for his brother is dead, and he is left alone. If any calamity should befall him along the way in which you go, then you would bring down my gray hair with sorrow to the grave.' (Genesis 42:36–38)

We then read that when Joseph's brothers came back and told Jacob that his son Joseph was alive after all:

'Jacob's heart stood still, because he did not believe them.'
(Genesis 45:26)

It was all too much for this elderly man, for his time of grief had been long and he had yet to walk out of the shadows. It is interesting to note that when Jacob saw the chariots and carts, which Joseph had sent to fetch him:

'The spirit of Jacob their father revived. Then Israel said, "It is enough. Joseph my son is alive. I will go and see him before I die." ' (Genesis 45:27, 28)

It will be necessary to give people as much time as they need in order to walk through their valley of pain, although there will also be the right moment to encourage them onto the next stage of ministry or restoration. It will all depend on the depth of the pain and the sensitivity of the person involved. For example, Jim had gone through bereavement three years earlier, having lost his wife through cancer, and some in the church felt that he had walked in pain for long enough. They tried to jolly him out of it, but in his case it was too soon. He needed more time. Conversely, Sarah's marriage had broken up eighteen months previously. She had received quite a lot of prayer ministry and was surrounded by loving friends who allowed her to talk through her pain and loneliness. There came a day when she felt that God was telling her to move on into the future, only to find that some in the church tried to hold her back! They continued to suffocate her with sympathy and to accuse her of being in denial if she didn't want to 'wallow' for a few more months. Every person is unique and therefore will need as much, or as little, time as is necessary and the wise and discerning person will know when the time has come to move forward.

It also, of course, takes time for a person to walk away from the sinful behaviour patterns which they may have learnt in response to their pain. They may, through ministry, have confessed and repented of them, but it is OK for them to have some time relearning new ones, without being judged too harshly. It is invaluable, if during this time a good friend is at hand in case they fall back into their old ways, as they may be tempted to do, and to encourage them to continue to walk forward.

Practical help is also indispensable to those who are hurting, especially if they are in the position where they are virtually unable to help themselves, as was true in the case of Elijah. He was driven into the wilderness by a woman's threatening words:

> *'So let the gods do to me, and more also, if I do not make your life as the life of one of them by tomorrow about this time.'*
>
> (1 Kings 19:2)

(Elijah had had the false prophets of Baal executed by the sword.) These words had sent Elijah into a spiral of despair, and ended up with him running for his life into the wilderness. Elijah was exhausted, depressed and in despair, and part of his restoration to wholeness was the cake which the angel baked for him, as well as the deep sleep, which he so badly needed.

Emotional hurt and pain can be so very draining in every way – physically, mentally and spiritually; so the offer of practical help can be invaluable. A house cleaned, a gift of a cake or a pie, a trip to the New Forest, a game of golf or a visit to a football match speaks volumes to the wounded person. It says: 'You care.' I asked one lady what had been the most healing, practical thing that anyone had ever done for her as she came through to restoration. Her answer was 'When they responded to my need for a godly hug in a positive way, without any sense of abuse or condemnation.' She had felt so affirmed and encouraged. She was also aware of the dangers of transference and always asked for a hug either from another lady or from an elderly couple with whom she felt safe.

When the disciples were distraught after Jesus' death on the Cross, thinking that they had lost Him forever, Jesus shows practical help and concern for them. There on the banks of the Sea of Tiberias, Jesus cooks breakfast for them. Knowing that they would be grief-stricken and heartbroken and probably not having eaten much food during the last day or two, he calls out:

'Come and eat breakfast.'   (John 21:12)

The steadfast love of the Lord never ceases. He knows our frame and He remembereth that we are dust! We likewise need to remember that our brothers and sisters may also be in need of such practical support, as they walk out of their hurt and pain.

In the whole area of coping with pain, whilst in the process of healing, we may like to suggest that people write down their thoughts and feelings, as a way of expressing what is sometimes inexpressible. Maybe suggest that they share their deepest thoughts with a beloved pet, if they are not yet ready to share with a human being. A friend of mine used the ear of an old teddy-bear, that was found in the back of the toy cupboard and which was given a new lease of life as the lady walked and talked through her pain into restoration.

Creative activities are also a tremendous avenue of restoration. As we have already seen, when the heart is in sorrow, the spirit also may become broken. We need to find ways for the wounded person's spirit to be healed and nurtured, in order that the person's human spirit will be able to function strongly again and strengthen and nurture the rest of the person. A walk in the countryside, gardening, rambling on the fells, painting, sculpting, creating music are all aesthetic activities which will help to nurture the spirit and feed restoration and health into the wounded soul.

A **rhema word** is also a priceless possession during the restoration process, as much as it is during ministry, as Hannah found to her great delight when Eli the priest spoke to her in the midst of her deep distress. A *rhema* word is a word, given to you from Scripture, either through another person or directly by the Holy Spirit as you read the Bible. Hannah was, you remember, taunted by her husband's other wife, Peninnah, because she had no children. Hannah, at that point was *'A woman of sorrowful spirit'* (1 Samuel 1:15). And then Eli, the priest spoke to her and gave her a word:

> *'Go in peace, and the God of Israel grant your petition which you have asked of Him.'*   (1 Samuel 1:17)

The transformation was instant and apparent:

> *'So the woman went her way and ate, and her face was no longer sad.'*   (1 Samuel 1:18)

I remember the deep peace which settled on the spirit of a lady I was ministering to, into the whole area of abuse and betrayal by her husband. God suddenly spoke deep into her spirit specifically and directly. Jane was feeling very rejected and isolated in her pain and could see no hope or encouragement on the horizon. Another lady, who was ministering alongside me, suddenly said: 'I believe the Lord wants you to receive this word,' and she turned to Jane with the Scripture:

> *'For your Maker is your husband,*
> *The LORD of hosts is His name;*
> *And your Redeemer is the Holy One of Israel;*
> *He is called the God of the whole earth.*
> *For the LORD has called you*
> *Like a woman forsaken and grieved in spirit,*
> *Like a youthful wife when you were refused.'*

(Isaiah 54:5, 6)

The transformation was immediate and apparent. What had happened? I believe the word was taken by the Holy Spirit, through revelation, deep into her human spirit and it was sealed there as a deposit of hope.

A similar instance was when a lady, whom I will call Margaret, was sharing her agony with us. An agony which she had felt as a little five-year-old, on discovering that her pet dog was missing on her return from school. It was her practice to fling off her coat and rush out into the garden and romp with her dog as soon as she got home. Great was the joy which they felt, and screams of delight could be heard, as they greeted one other on the lawn. She was a rather lonely little girl, with no friends of her own age, and this dog 'Wuffie' was everything to her: friend, companion, and playmate. Unbeknown to Margaret the dog was ill with kidney trouble. Wuffie had been taken to the vet that day for treatment, but had had to be put to sleep. Her parents were extremely sad, especially for their little daughter, but Margaret herself was inconsolable.

In the midst of our praying she felt that the Lord spoke to her and encouraged her to turn to Isaiah 51:3, a reference which she was not overly familiar with. The passage read:

> *'For the LORD will comfort Zion,*
> *He will comfort all her waste places;*
> *He will make her wilderness like Eden,*
> *And her desert like the garden of the LORD;*
> *Joy and gladness will be found in it,*
> *Thanksgiving and the voice of melody.'*

At first she was overcome to think that the Lord would speak so specifically to her, and especially that He had given the Scripture directly to her, rather than through us. This was important to Margaret, who reckoned that she never heard directly from the Lord, because she wasn't good enough. (Her low self-image was one of the reasons why she had difficulty in making close friends.) That word, from Scripture, brought a release of tears of joy as well as of the buried pain, and it continued to sustain her faith for many weeks and months, as she walked through into her healing and restoration.

Restoration Through the Human Spirit

If it is true that the spirit can be broken because of sorrow within the heart, it is probably also true that the spirit, when it is strong, will bring restoration into the heart. According to Proverbs 18:14:

'The spirit of a man will sustain him in sickness, but who can bear a broken spirit?'

Thus we are encouraged to believe that our human spirit is meant to sustain us in the midst of our infirmities and pain. For a greater understanding of the functions of our human spirit, a fuller coverage is given in my book, *Healing the Human Spirit* (published by New Wine Press). Suffice it to say that one of the functions of our spirit is to comfort and strengthen our bodies and soul. The stronger therefore that our human spirit becomes, the greater will its facility be to strengthen and feed life into the heart, soul and body of the person. There are a number of ways to strengthen the spirit:
- feeding on the word of God will empower the spirit;
- worshipping will build up the spirit – both personal and corporate devotions;
- praying;
- taking part in the Sacraments.

Thus, the **Holy Spirit the Comforter** is enabled through **our spirit** to pour comfort, strength and the Balm of Gilead into our hearts until the restoration process is complete.

To all of you, then, who are emotionally wounded and heartbroken and who are in the process of walking into your healing, I would encourage you to hold on to the promises of God. For it is still true that He speaks today and that He speaks to you. Take hold of His promise that:

> ' "I will restore health to you
> And heal you of your wounds," says the Lord.'
>
> (Jeremiah 30:17)

May this be to you a *rhema* word that will be seeded into your spirit and bring wholeness into your soul.